More! Instant Bible Lessons for Preschoolers

God Helps Me

Pamela J. Kuhn

These pages may be copied.
Permission is granted to the buyer of this book to
photocopy student materials in this book for
use with Sunday school or Bible teaching classes.

Rainbow Publishers

Rainbow Publishers • P.O. Box 261129 • San Diego, CA 92196
www.rainbowpublishers.com

To my dearest Carli and Olivia:
You sweet little girls are truly great nieces. It is like seeing the infant and toddler stages of your
mommy all over! I pray you will grow to love Jesus as you follow Him every day. All my love,
Auntie Pam.

MORE! INSTANT BIBLE LESSONS FOR PRESCHOOLERS: GOD HELPS ME
©2009 by Rainbow Publishers, first printing
ISBN 10: 1-58411-070-8
ISBN 13: 978-1-58411-070-5
Rainbow reorder# RB36856
RELIGION / Christian Ministry / Children

Rainbow Publishers
P.O. Box 261129
San Diego, CA 92196
www.rainbowpublishers.com

Interior Illustrator: Hallie Gillett
Cover Illustrator: Tammie Lyon

Certified Chain of Custody
SUSTAINABLE Promoting Sustainable
FORESTRY Forest Management
INITIATIVE
www.sfiprogram.org

Scriptures are from the *Holy Bible: New International Version* (North American Edition), ©1973, 1978, 1984 by the
International Bible Society. Used by permission of Zondervan Bible Publishers.

Printed in the United States of America

Contents

Introduction

Wecome to *God Helps Me*, a book packed full with useful lesson activities for your preschoolers. You'll find the lively Bible stories and kid-friendly activities make it easy to teach about all the traits God helps children to have, such as kindness, fairness, responsibility, and trustworthiness. Engage your students with active games and songs, set to familiar melodies, along with age-appropriate puzzles and worksheets. You'll find clear directions and lists of materials for the crafts and snacks, so you'll always be ready to go.

Each of the first eight chapters includes a Bible story, memory verse and numerous activities to help reinforce the lessons about the ways God helps you. An additional chapter contains projects that can be used anytime throughout the study or at the end to review the lessons. Teacher aids, including bulletin board ideas and discussion starters, are sprinkled throughout the book.

The most exciting aspect of the *More Instant Bible Lessons for Preschoolers* series is its flexibility. You can easily adapt these lessons to a Sunday School hour, a children's church service, a Wednesday night Bible study, a Christian school classroom or family home use. And, because there is a variety of reproducible ideas from which to choose, you will enjoy creating a class session that is best for your group — whether large or small, beginning or advanced, active or studious.

This book is written to add fun and uniqueness to learning about the ways God helps you. Teaching children is exciting and rewarding, especially when you successfully share God's Word and its principles with your students. *More Instant Bible Lessons for Preschoolers* will help you accomplish that goal. Blessings on you as your students learn how God helps them.

How to Use This Book

Each chapter begins with a Bible story for you to read to your class, followed by discussion questions. Then, use any or all of the activities in the chapter to help drive home the message of that lesson. Each activity is tagged with one of the icons below, so you can quickly flip through the chapter and select the projects you need. Simply cut off the teacher instructions on the pages and duplicate as desired.

| craft | skit | teacher help | bulletin board | activity |

| puzzle | action song | song | game | snack |

Chapter 1
God Helps Me to Be Compassionate

Memory Verse

Clothe yourselves with compassion.
Colossians 3:12

Story to Share
Dorcas Shows Compassion

In and out, in and out. Dorcas carefully pushed the needle into the fabric of the coat she was making, then pulled it out. The coat was for Levi, Naomi's little boy. Levi's father had died, and Naomi didn't have money for new clothes for her children. So Dorcas was happy she could help Naomi and Levi.

As Levi watched the fabric turn into a coat, he smiled. He liked to watch Dorcas sew.

Dorcas saw Levi's smile. "You look happy, Levi," she said.

"I am happy," Levi told her. "You are the best sewer in the world. My mommy said you are the most loving lady she knows, and I think so, too."

Dorcas smiled and said, "Sewing is what God gave me to do. I don't know how to cook well, and I'm not a very good teacher."

Levi looked at the needle in her hand. "But your needle goes right where it belongs."

"Yes, it does," agreed Dorcas.

The next afternoon, instead of Dorcas sewing in the sun, there were women, crying.

"What's wrong?" Levi asked as he pulled at his mom's dress.

"Dorcas is dead," she said to Levi, between sobs. "What are we going to do without this compassionate woman?"

It seemed like all the women were talking at once, telling their stories of Dorcas's generosity. Then Levi saw Peter in the crowd.

Peter walked into Dorcas's room and knelt by her body. "Get up, Dorcas," he said quietly.

Dorcas opened her eyes and sat up. When she walked out to her place in the sun, she was holding Levi's coat. The women were so happy to see her alive and well that they raised their hands and praised God. But Levi was happiest of all.

— Based on Acts 9:32-42

Discussion Questions

1. Dorcas was compassionate. She liked to help others. What can you do to help your friend or mother?

2. What should we say to those who help us?

7

puzzle

What You Need

• duplicated page
• pencils
• crayons
• small crackers

What to Do

1. Duplicate a worksheet for each child.
2. Instruct the children to count the coats in each box and write the number in the square.
3. Allow the children to color the pictures.
4. Give each child 21 crackers.

What to Say

Lay a cracker on each coat Dorcas made. She used the talent God gave her to show compassion to others. What talent do you have that could be used to help others?

Compassionate

How Many Garments?

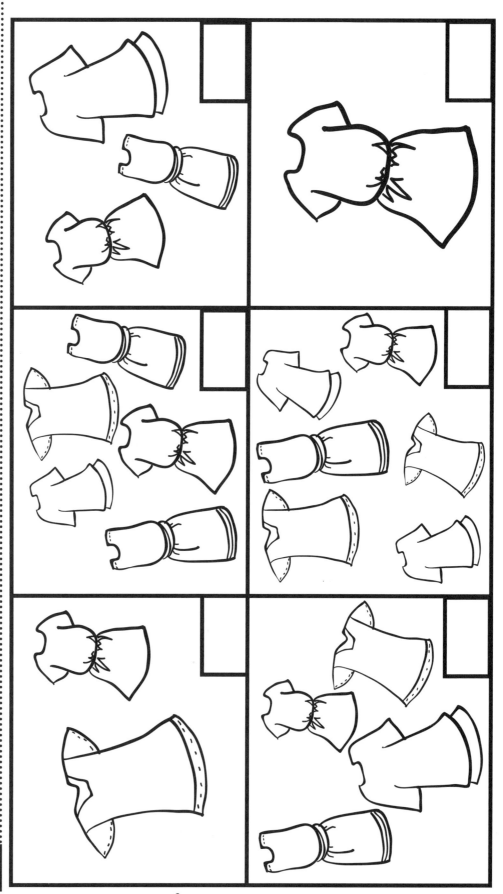

Dorcas' Story Book

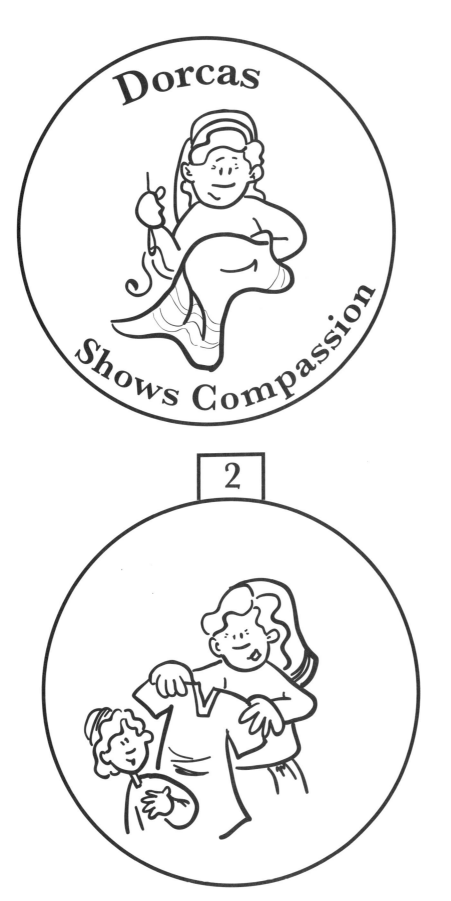

craft
. . . .
What You Need
• storybook pages
• crayons
• glue

What to Do
1. Before class, make a picture book for yourself.
2. Duplicate and cut out a set of storybook pages for each child.
3. Read the story on page 7 to the children.
4. Allow the children to color the pages.
5. Assist the children in assembling the books. For each book, fold the tabs towards the pictures. Glue the back side of the #2 tab to the back of the cover. Glue the back side of the #3 tab to the back of picture 2 and so on.

What to Say
Listen carefully while I tell the story. Then each of you will make a book so you can have turns telling the story.

Continued on next page...

Compassionate

Verse Race

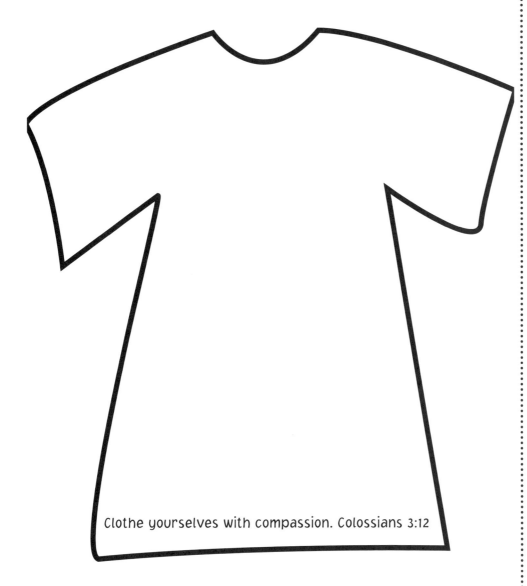

Clothe yourselves with compassion. Colossians 3:12

game

What You Need
- duplicated page
- clothesline
- spring-type clothespins
- basket
- fabric and trim scraps
- buttons
- glue
- crayons
- card stock

What to Do
1. Duplicate and cut out a coat for each child on card stock.
2. Hang a clothesline between two chairs (low enough that the children can reach it).
3. Place the clothespins in a basket in the middle of the line.
4. Allow the children to color their coats and decorate them with fabric and buttons.
5. Form two teams and instruct the team members to stand in two lines. You should stand by the clothesline.
6. The first child in

Continued at left...

Continued from right...
each line should run to the clothesline, say the memory verse to you, grab a clothespin and pin his or her robe to the line. Then those students should run back to their lines and touch the hands of the next students in line. The team who finishes first wins.

7. Optional: If you have a small class or want to have a non-competitive game, use one team. You can use a stopwatch to see how long it takes to "hang out the wash."

Compassionate

A Seamstress Snack

snack

What You Need

- duplicated page
- card stock
- shoestring licorice
- refrigerated sugar cookie dough
- clear, self-stick plastic

What to Do

1. Duplicate the spools to card stock, one per child. Cover the spools with clear plastic and cut them out.
2. Slice the sugar cookie dough. Before baking, poke two holes in each one to look like button holes.
3. Give each child two licorice strings, a spool and cookie.
4. Assist each child in wrapping the licorice around the spool to look like thread, and tying a piece of licorice through the cookie button holes.

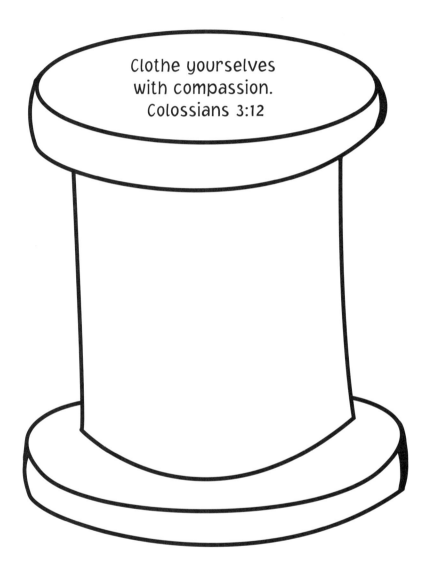

Clothe yourselves with compassion. Colossians 3:12

I can show compassion to you when you are hungry by providing a snack. But what can we do to show compassion to hungry children in other countries? (give money for food to feed them)

Compassionate

number the Pictures

Clothe yourselves with compassion.
Colossians 3:12

puzzle

What You Need
- duplicated page
- crayons

What to Do
1. Duplicate a worksheet for each child.
2. Instruct the children to look at the pictures. Discuss each picture, then ask, "Which picture comes first?"
3. Instruct the children to draw pictures of themselves showing compassion in the worksheets' final box.

Compassionate

13

puzzle

What You Need
- duplicated page
- crayons

What to Do
1. Duplicate a worksheet for each child.
2. Instruct the children to look at the first picture. Read the words under the picture. Allow the children to decide if the words are true about Dorcas. If they are, the students should color that picture.
3. Continue with the other descriptions.

Compassionate

All About Dorcas

brought back to life by Peter

cooked for her friends

told stories about Jesus

sewed for the poor

was very old

Dorcas

showed love and compassion

had friends who praised God for her

14

Watch Me Sew

In and out.
In and out.
Dorcas's needle never quit.
In and out.
In and out.
Showing compassion
bit by bit.

craft

What You Need
- duplicated page
- card stock
- hole punch
- yarn
- glue

What to Do
1. Duplicate the needle to card stock and cut out one for each child. Punch holes in each needle for its "eye."
2. Give each child a length of yarn.
3. Instruct the children to fold the needles on the dashed lines.
4. Show how to thread yarn through the top hole, pulling a little ways into the fold. Allow the children to glue the needle backs together.
5. Say the poem with the children while they pretend to be sewing.

Compassionate

craft

What You Need
- duplicated page
- crochet thread
- glue
- fabric scraps
- construction paper

What to Do
1. Duplicate and cut out a needle for each child. Punch a hole for the eye of each needle.
2. Trace the coat pattern onto fabric scraps and cut out one for each child.
3. Allow each child to choose a color of construction paper for his or her poster.
4. Instruct the children to glue their fabric coats to their construction paper sheets.
5. Show how to insert a length of crochet thread through the needle and glue it to the coat.

Compassionate

Compassion Poster

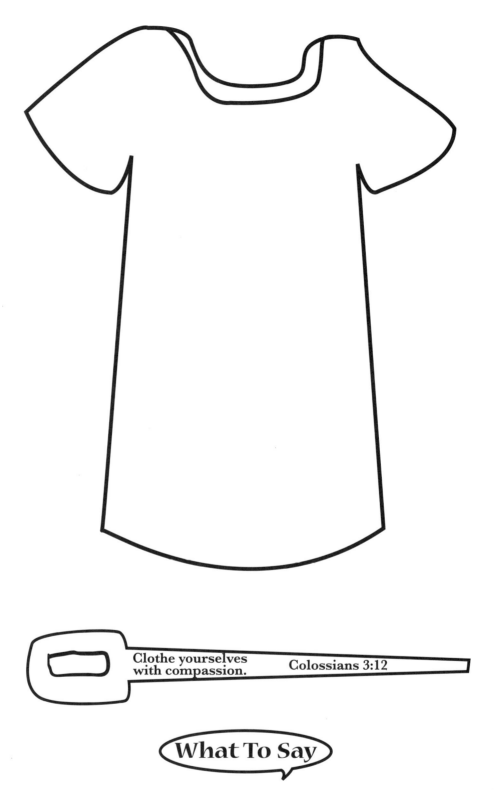

Clothe yourselves with compassion.   Colossians 3:12

What To Say

Just as we make sure we put on our clothes, socks and shoes each day, we need to make sure we have compassion in our hearts. You might not be able to sew, but you can pick flowers to cheer a sick neighbor, take a bandage to a friend who is hurt or give a hug to your mother when she's tired.

Chapter 2
God Helps Me to Be Fair

Memory Verse

Do what is right and just.
Proverbs 21:3

Story to Share
Dear Timothy

Little Timothy was a happy child. Even though his father didn't believe in Jesus, Timothy's grandmother Lois and his mother, Eunice, were Christians. One of Timothy's favorite times of the day was when his mother would tell him stories about Jesus.

"Jesus took the five small loaves of bread and two dried fish from the little boy. This tiny lunch fed 5,000 people, Timothy," she said one day as she taught Timothy about Jesus' miracles.

Timothy wished he could have been there to see that miracle.

"Tell me another story, Mommy," Timothy begged.

As he heard his mother's stories of Jesus, Timothy realized he wanted to be a follower of Jesus.

"I believe You are the Son of God," Timothy prayed one day. "I want to belong to You."

Timothy began studying the Scriptures to learn everything he could about God. He became a sincere disciple.

One day the missionary Paul came to visit. Paul was surprised to see how dedicated young Timothy was. Paul was impressed with Timothy's knowledge of the Scriptures and with his deep love for the stories of Jesus.

"Come with me, Timothy," Paul said. "I need a helper on my missionary journeys."

Traveling with Paul taught Timothy even more about the God he loved. Soon Paul appointed Timothy as bishop of the church at Ephesus.

One day Paul wrote Timothy a letter.

"Dear Timothy," the letter began, "don't forget the teaching and stories your mother and grandmother taught you. Be fair. Don't show favor."

Paul was Timothy's hero. Timothy knew that Paul taught only the truth. Timothy asked God to help him to be fair and to follow all of Paul's instructions to do only what was right and fair.

— Based on 1 Timothy 5

Discussion Questions

1. Who told Timothy to be fair?
2. How can you be fair with your friends?

Be Fair Wind Hanging

craft

What You Need
- duplicated page
- crepe paper
- glue
- crayons
- yarn

What to Do
1. Duplicate a bee and set of letters for each child.
2. Cut crepe paper into 6" strips. You will need four for each child.
3. Allow the children to color the bee and letters.
4. Instruct each child to glue a letter on each crepe paper strip.
5. Assist the children in gluing the crepe paper strips to the bottoms of their bees.
6. Go around and attach a yarn hanger to the back of each bee.

Fair

Bees are fair to each other. Worker bees guard the entrance to the hives, fan their wings to keep the hive cool and collect nectar to make honey. All of the bees do the jobs assigned to them. One way you can be fair to your family is to do what your parents ask you to do. God is happy when we are fair.

Pick a Bible

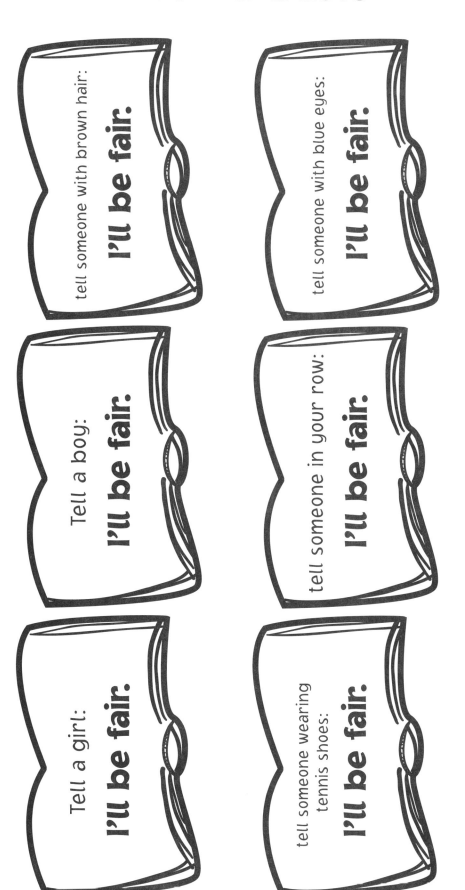

tell someone with brown hair:
I'll be fair:

tell someone with blue eyes:
I'll be fair:

Tell a boy:
I'll be fair:

tell someone in your row:
I'll be fair:

Tell a girl:
I'll be fair:

tell someone wearing tennis shoes:
I'll be fair:

game

What You Need
- duplicate page
- bag

What to Do
1. Duplicate and cut out the Bibles. Make sure you have one Bible for each child.
2. Place the Bibles in a bag.
3. Allow each child to pick a Bible. Assist in reading the commands on the Bibles, then let each child do what the Bible commands.

What to Say
After all the Bibles have been chosen, say, "Timothy learned how to be fair when his mom told him stories from God's Word, the Bible. You can learn how to be fair when you pay attention to Bible stories, too."

Fair

Good Friend Award

song

What You Need
• duplicated page
• yarn
• crayons
• glue

What to Do
1. Duplicate and cut out an award for each child.
2. For each child, form a circle with an 18" piece of yarn and tie the ends together.
3. Allow the children to color their awards.
4. Assist each child in folding an award on the dashed lines, sandwiching the yarn inside the fold to make a necklace. Allow the students to glue the front and back circles together.
5. Sing the song to the tune of "Jingle Bells." When you sing the last line, each child should give his or her award to another.

Fair

Just Be Fair

Just be fair, just be fair,
Paul warned Tim-o-thy.
He wrote the letter to his friend
That he shared with you and me.

Just be fair, just be fair,
You can do it, too.
Treat your friend in an honest way,
And your friendship will be true.

Good Friend Award

Do what is right and just. Proverbs 21:3

Just be fair, just be fair,
Paul warned Tim-o-thy.
He wrote the letter to his friend
That he shared with you and me.

Just be fair, just be fair,
You can do it, too.
Treat your friend in an honest way,
And your friendship will be true.

Busy Bee Snack

Ingredients

- ¼ cup powdered sugar
- ¼ cup honey
- ¼ cup peanut butter
- ¼ cup crispy rice cereal
- ¼ cup raisins
- chocolate sprinkles
- sliced almonds

I will

be fair.

snack

What You Need

- duplicated page
- yellow paper
- Pop Dots® (see note)
- stapler
- ingredients, at left

What to Do

1. Mix together the sugar, honey, peanut butter, cereal and raisins. Shape the mix into bee bodies (ovals) and roll in sprinkles. Push an almond in each side for wings.
2. Duplicate a bee and hive to yellow paper for each child.
3. Assist the children in printing their names on the lowest sections of their hives.
4. Instruct the children to glue the tabs of the hives together so the hives stand.
5. Allow the children to attach Pop Dots® to the backs of their bees and attach the other

Continued at left...

Continued from right...

  sides of the Pop Dots® to the hives.
6. Use this hive place card to mark each child's place at the snack table.
7. Serve the bee snacks.
8. Allow the children to take home the place cards as reminders to be fair during meals.

Note: Pop Dots® are foam circles with adhesive on both sides to make items look "3D." They arc found where scrapbooking supplies are sold.

Fair

Cleaning Up

What You Need
- duplicated page
- crayons
- glue

What to Do

1. Duplicate a worksheet and cut out a set of cleaning tools for each child.
2. Allow the children to color the pictures.
3. Assist the children in gluing the broom in the boy's hand and the waste can beside him. Assist the children in gluing the rag in the girl's hand and the spray cleaner on the table.
4. Discuss the chores that need to be done for the room to be clean again.

What to Say

How can you be fair when you and your friend made a mess? (by helping to clean up) When you do your share of the work, you are fair. God likes it when we are fair to each other.

Fair

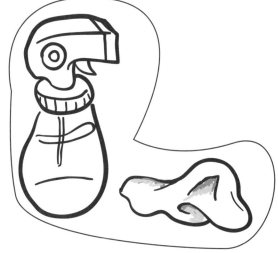

BEE-ing Fair

puzzle

What You Need
• duplicated page
• crayons

What to Do
1. Duplicate a coloring sheet for each child.
2. Instruct the children to color all the spaces with the word "fair" yellow, and the spaces with the word "bee" blue.

What to Say
A bee is fair when it leaves some nectar for another bee. We can be fair when we take one cookie and leave the other for a friend. God wants us to be fair.

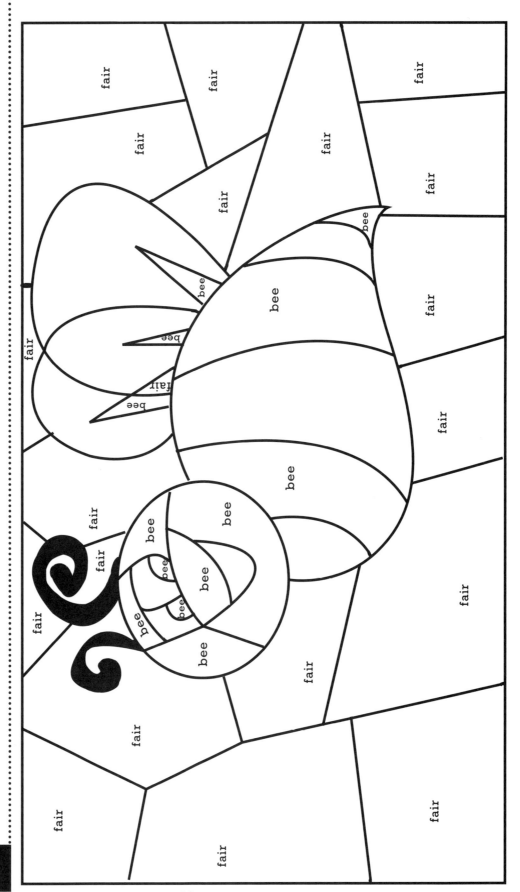

Timothy's Letter

Do what is right and just.
Proverbs 21:3

Continued from right...
on his or her envelope. If time permits, allow the children to decorate their envelopes.

What to Say
The envelope has your name on it. Even though Paul wrote his letter to Timothy, God wanted it in His Word so we can read it and learn to be fair, too.

puzzle

What You Need
• duplicated page
• crayons
• envelopes

What to Do
1. Duplicate a puzzle for each child.
2. Allow the children to color their puzzles.
3. Read the Scripture on the puzzle. Encourage the children to repeat the verse as they color the puzzle.
4. Go around and cut out the puzzle on the solid lines (or allow the children to cut with safety scissors).
5. Explain to the children that when Timothy was a boy, the Scriptures were written on scrolls rather than in books as we have today.
6. Allow the children to put together their puzzles. Repeat the memory verse.
7. Give each child an envelope in which to take home the letter puzzle. Print each child's name

Continued at left...

Fair

25

A Story to Read

puzzle

What You Need
- duplicated page
- construction paper
- glue
- crayons

What to Do
1. Duplicate a story for each child.
2. Cut construction paper 1" larger than the story on each side.
3. Allow the children to color the pictures.
4. Instruct the children to glue their stories to construction paper and fold over the construction paper to make a book.
5. Read the story to the children, stopping to allow them to "read" the pictures.

Fair

---

   fed **5,000** people with

the little 's lunch.

wrote a to

"**B** fair," told him. Do what is right and just."

John 6:1-15 and 1 Timothy 5

 's mother and grandmother told him about

loved hearing the stories. His favorite story

 was about the little

 who gave his lunch of

 5 and 2

Chapter 3

God Helps Me to Be Forgiving

📖 Memory Verse

Forgive, and you will be forgiven.
Luke 6:37

📖 Story to Share
David Chooses Forgiveness

Saul was the king at the time David killed Goliath and saved the people of Israel from the Philistines. Saul was happy that the Philistines lost, but when King Saul returned home, the women were singing and dancing. When King Saul heard their song's words, he got angry.

"King Saul has killed his thousands," the women sang, "but David has killed his ten thousands."

From that day on, King Saul was jealous of David. He was afraid David would take the kingdom away from him.

David had to hide from King Saul. So he took some of his men and they hid in caves and forests.

One day, David heard that King Saul and his army were looking for him. He hid deep in a cave.

As David waited, he saw that King Saul had grown tired and was lying on the ground near the entrance of the cave. There were no soldiers near him.

"Hurry," whispered one of David's men. "Here's your chance to kill him."

David thought about all the mean things that King Saul had done to him, and how he had to live in caves because of King Saul.

But David knew God would not be pleased if he was mean back at King Saul. Instead David just snuck up behind King Saul and carefully cut off a piece of King Saul's robe.

When King Saul awoke and left the cave, David secretly followed him. King Saul was carefully walking among the rocks on the hillside. David stood high above him and called, "King Saul!"

King Saul spun around in surprise. He watched as David bowed in respect. "Is that you, David?" the king asked.

"Yes," answered David. "Today I was close enough to kill you, but I couldn't kill the Lord's chosen king. I have chosen to forgive you instead."

King Saul never admitted his jealousy toward David. But David had chosen forgiveness and did not harm the king.

— Based on 1 Samuel 24

❓❓ Discussion Questions

1. Did David do anything wrong to Saul to make him angry?
2. Can you forgive a friend who is angry with you?

craft

What You Need
• duplicated page
• fabric
• crayons
• glue
• magnet tape

What to Do
1. Duplicate a page for each child.
2. Draw around King Saul's robe for a pattern. Cut a robe out of fabric for each child. Cut a section from the bottom of each robe.
3. Allow the children to color their King Sauls and Davids.
4. Tell the children to glue the fabric robe to King Saul.
5. Assist each child in attaching a piece of magnet tape to the back of the cut out section of fabric and to the place on Saul's robe. Attach magnet tape to David's hand so he can pull the fabric away.
6. Complete a figure set for yourself before class. Use the figures to tell the story.

Forgiving

Bible Story Figures

Find Your Partners

puzzle

What You Need
- duplicated page
- colored paper
- clear, self-stick plastic
- sack

What to Do
1. Duplicate puzzles to different colors of paper (you will need one puzzle piece for each child).
2. Cover the puzzles with clear plastic.
3. Cut apart all the pieces and put them in a sack.
4. Allow each child to choose a piece.
5. At the "go" signal, those with the same color puzzle piece should group and try to put their puzzles together. When each team's puzzle is complete, they should announce, "We forgive you."

Forgiving

The Forgiving Reply

activity

What You Need
- duplicated page
- crayons

What to Do
1. Duplicate a worksheet for each child.
2. Instruct the children to look at each picture. Read each word bubble to the children.
3. Instruct the children to color the happy face if the person in the picture made a forgiving reply. If it was an unforgiving reply, the children should color the frowning face.

Forgiving

Fit the Picture

puzzle

· · · · · · · · · · · ·

What You Need
- duplicated page
- crayons
- glue

What to Do
1. Duplicate and cut out a worksheet and picture set for each child.
2. Allow the children to color the scenes and pictures.
3. Instruct each child to find the picture that fits each empty spot and glue it to the worksheet.

What to Say
It doesn't matter if the person who hurt us is big or little, God still wants us to forgive. Say this with me, "Big or little, I will forgive. That's the way David chose to live."

Continued on next page...

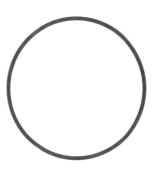

Forgiving

Chalkboard Object Lesson

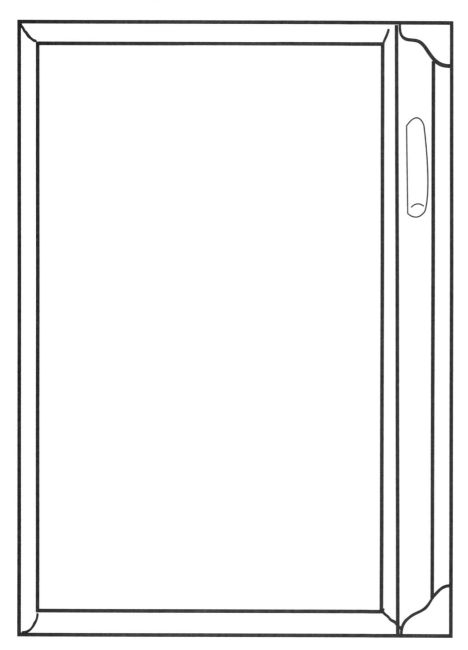

craft

What You Need
- duplicated page
- black construction paper
- white crayons
- glue
- chalkboard
- chalk
- eraser
- broken chalk pieces

What to Do
1. Duplicate and cut out a chalkboard for each child.
2. Trace the center of each chalkboard onto black construction paper and cut a piece for each child.
3. Allow each child to draw a big smiley face on the black paper using a white crayon.
4. Instruct the children to glue the black papers to the chalkboards and the pieces of chalk where indicated.

What To Say

Discuss things someone could do to hurt another. Write them on the (real) chalkboard. Ask a child what God wants us to do when people are unkind to us. (Forgive)

Choose a child to erase the chalkboard. Say, "When God forgives our sins, He never reminds us of them again. When we forgive others, we should never remind them of how they hurt us. Forgiveness wipes the slate clean and gives us a smile."

Forgiving

'F' is for Forgiving

snack

What You Need
• duplicated page
• edible fruit roll
• clear, self-stick plastic
• crayons

What to Do
1. Duplicate and cut out an "F" letter for each child.
2. Let the children color their letters.
3. Cover each letter with clear plastic. Let the children smooth the plastic onto the letter.
4. Give each child a fruit roll.
5. Instruct the children to follow the "F" with their fruit roll. Show how to roll up the length of the "F," then tear the remaining fruit roll into two pieces to lay on the legs of the letter.

What to Say
Forgiveness begins with the letter "F." Before you eat your fruit roll, let's thank Jesus for coming to forgive our sins.

Forgiving

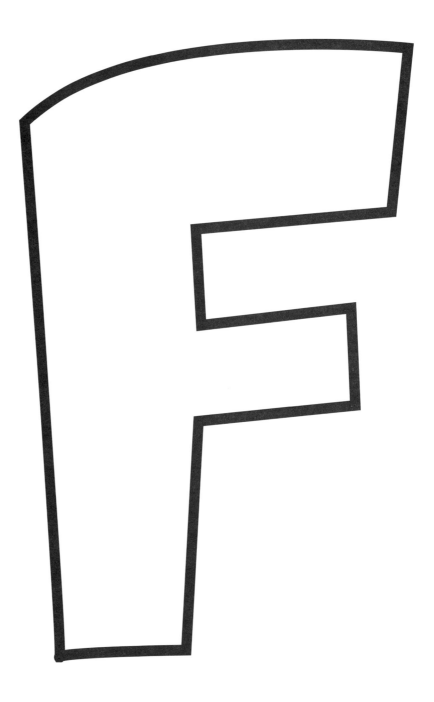

1-2-3-4 Giving

Who was king when David killed Goliath? (Saul)
Was King Saul happy the Philistines lost? (yes)
How did King Saul feel when he heard the song the women were singing? (angry)
Where did David hide from King Saul? (in caves and forests)
What was King Saul doing when David found him? (sleeping)
What did David's men want him to do to the king? (kill him)
What did David do?(cut off a piece of Saul's robe)
What did David choose to do instead of harming King Saul? (forgive him)

game

What You Need
• duplicated page
• basket

What to Do
1. Duplicate and cut out three sets of numbers and the "Giving" box.
2. Place the numbers and words in the basket.
3. Divide the children into teams. The first team answers a question. If the answer is correct, they draw a number or word.
4. The goal is to get the numbers 1, 2, 3 and 4, as well as the "Giving" box.
5. If a team draws a number or word they do not need, they must give it to the opposite team.

What to Say
How many times do you think you need to forgive somebody? When Jesus was asked this question His answer was 70 x 7. That's a lot of times! We should always forgive others.

Forgiving

"I Forgive You" Song

song

What You Need
- duplicated page
- fabric
- glue

What to Do
1. Duplicate and cut out a song sheet for each child.
2. Cut the fabric the size of the song sheet.
3. Allow the children to glue their fabric to the backs of their song sheets.
4. Sing the song to the tune of "Zacchaeus." Encourage the children to hold up the fabric sides when they sing, "I forgive you."

King Saul was a jealous king,
and a jealous king was he.

He tried to hurt and kill David,
'twas as jealous as could be.

But David forgave
and spared Saul's life,
cut a piece of robe with his knife.

(Spoken) And he said,
"Saul, I've forgiven you!

"It's what my God wants me to do.
It's what my God wants me to do."

Forgiving

Chapter 4
God Helps Me to Be A Good Citizen

Memory Verse

Even a child is known by his actions.
Proverbs 20:11

Story to Share
Take Care of the Earth

When God decided to create the earth, He worked on it for six days. God wanted it to be beautiful – and it was!

God used the color blue to create the sky and the oceans. He included lots of green when He created grass, trees and flower stems. He colored the ground and tree trunks brown. Then God splashed a bit of color everywhere when He made red, purple, yellow, orange and pink flowers.

God loved the colorful earth. He said, "It is good."

The earth was full of color, and God wanted people to help Him enjoy the beautiful world. "I will make a man – in my image," God said.

So God made Adam to enjoy the world.

"Adam," God said, "I want you to take care of My earth. Clean the earth, water the flowers to keep them beautiful and prune the fruit trees so they will continue to bear fruit."

Adam said, "I will be a good citizen of the earth." Adam liked to eat the apples and peaches, and he remembered that God wanted him to keep the trees trimmed. When Adam saw trash on the ground, he picked it up. He wanted to keep God's world beautiful.

Many years later, King David wrote in the Psalms, "The earth belongs to God." God allows us to live on His earth and enjoy its beauty, but we are commanded to take care of it. We need to keep the earth neat, fruitful and beautiful – just as Adam did in obedience to God.

— Based on Genesis 1 and 2

Discussion Questions

1. What does God want us to do with the earth?
2. What can you do when you see trash in your neighborhood?

song

What You Need
• duplicated page
• crayons
• glue
• ribbon

What to Do
1. Duplicate and cut out a picture and two buckles for each child.
2. Cut the ribbon in 4" lengths.
3. Allow the children to color the pictures.
4. Assist each child in gluing a ribbon across each child in the picture, and gluing a buckle at the side of each belt.
5. Sing the song to the tune of "Deep and Wide."

What to Say
Being a good citizen means obeying the rules and laws of our country. What are some laws our country has made? (stop at stop sign, don't litter, wear a seatbelt when riding in a vehicle)

Good Citizen

"Seatbelt" Song

Buckle up,
Buckle up,
There's a rule that tells us, "Buckle up."

Buckle up,
Buckle up,
God is happy when I'm a good citizen!

38

Garbage Police Badge

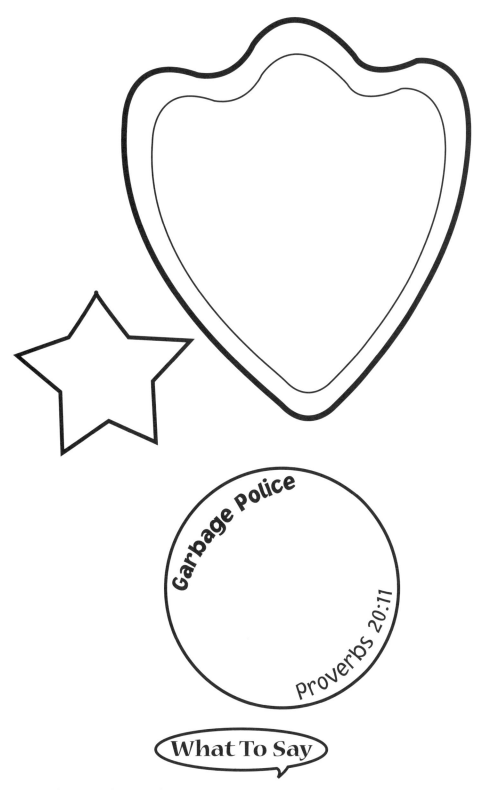

Garbage Police

Proverbs 20:11

What To Say

You can be a good citizen by picking up trash you see on the ground. Remember when you are finished with a gum wrapper, soft drink can or tissue to hold it until you are near a trash can. God wants us to be good citizens.

craft

What You Need
- duplicated page
- silver foil
- safety pins
- tape
- paper sacks

What to Do
1. Duplicate and cut out a set of badge pieces for each child, and one large star.
2. Use the star pattern to cut one from silver foil for each child.
3. Allow the children to glue the stars and "Garbage Police" circles on the badges.
4. Tape a safety pin to the back of each badge.
5. Pin a badge on each child.
6. Provide paper sacks for each child. Take a walk around the church grounds to pick up garbage.

Good Citizen

Popcorn Snack

snack
· · · · · · · · · · · ·

What You Need
- duplicated page
- envelopes
- stamps

What to Do
1. Duplicate a Popcorn Holder on neon paper for each child.
2. Assist the children in taping and folding the holders.
3. Allow each child to fill his holder.
4. Allow the children to enjoy their treats.

What to Say
Now that we have had our treat what should we do? (place trash in garbage can, wipe off table, wash hands) If we all work together, we'll have our chores finished quickly, and we will have a clean room again. God wants us to be good citizens.

Good Citizen

Good Citizen Snack

Proverbs 20:11

Recycle It!

game

What You Need
- duplicated page
- crayons
- clean trash can

What to Do
1. Duplicate a set of recycling products for each child.
2. Allow the children to color the pictures.
3. Calling each child by name, say, "[Hannah], it's time to recycle." That student should then take her products to the trash can and name each item as she throws it away. (Allow the children to retrieve them.)

What to Say
When we recycle, we are helping the earth. It is one way that we can help take care of the earth God made for us. Recycle to show you are a good citizen. God wants us to be good citizens.

Good Citizen

craft

What You Need
- duplicated page
- buttons
- glue
- fabric scraps
- construction paper

What to Do
1. Duplicate a Verse Poster for each child.
2. Show how to make a child on the poster using a button face, fabric scraps for clothes, etc.
3. Glue each poster on construction paper to make a frame.
4. Repeat the memory verse several times with the children.

"Child" Verse Poster

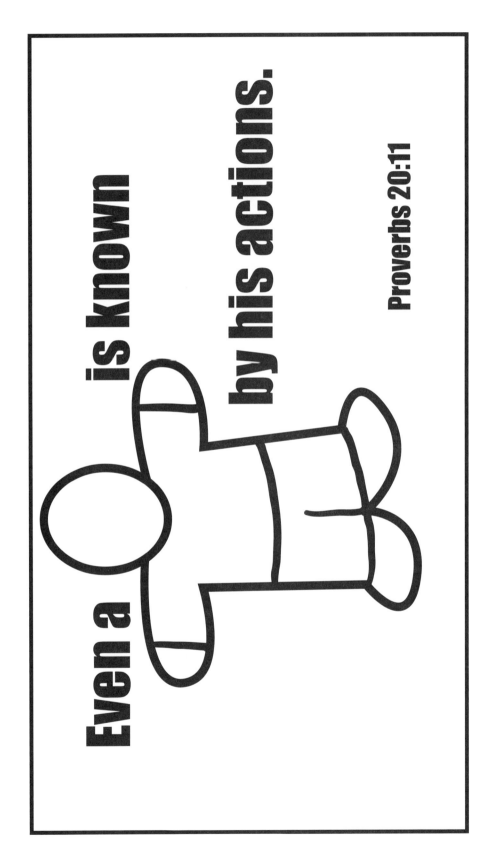

Even a is known by his actions. Proverbs 20:11

Good Citizen Game

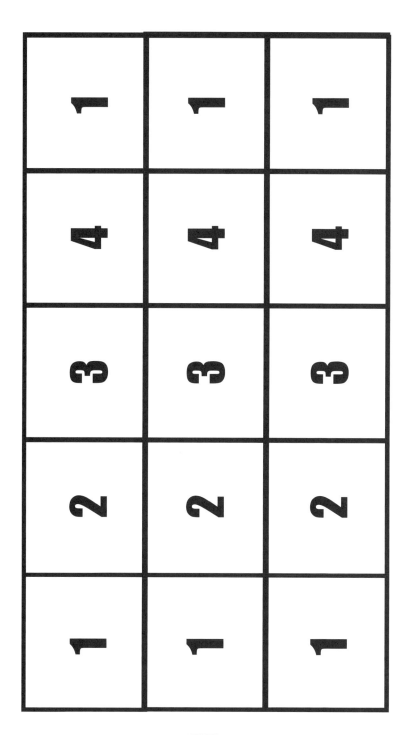

Sometimes we forget to be good citizens. When we know we've done something wrong, we just should say, "Oops!" and back up and do what's right. God wants us to be good citizens.

What You Need
• duplicated page
• buttons
• crayons

What to Do
1. Duplicate and cut out a game board and number set for each child.
2. Allow the children to color their game boards.
3. Have each child choose a partner and a button. (They will use only one of the game sets per pair in class, but they can take home the sets that they make.)
4. Instruct the children to place the cards upside down. The pairs should take turns choosing a card and moving the amount of spaces printed on it. Help the children read the commands.

Continued on next page...

Good Citizen

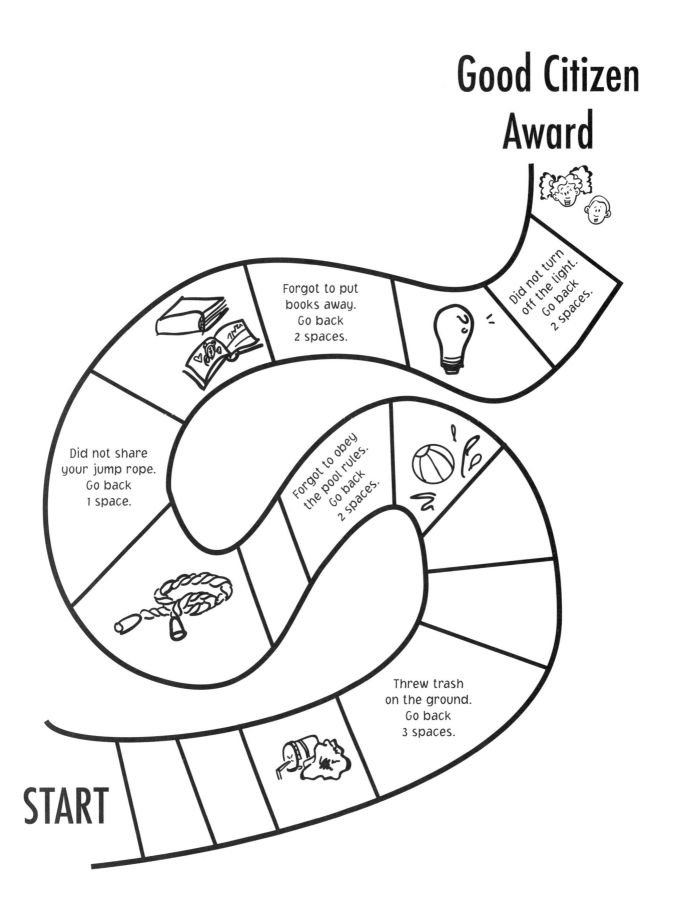

Good Citizen Award

Forgot to put books away. Go back 2 spaces.

Did not turn off the light. Go back 2 spaces.

Did not share your jump rope. Go back 1 space.

Forgot to obey the pool rules. Go back 2 spaces.

Threw trash on the ground. Go back 3 spaces.

START

Turn It Off!

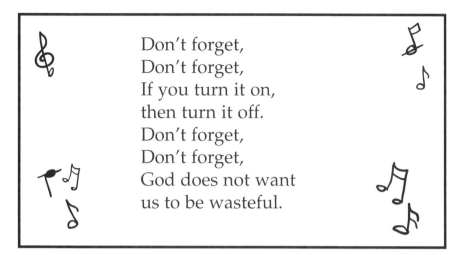

> Don't forget,
> Don't forget,
> If you turn it on,
> then turn it off.
> Don't forget,
> Don't forget,
> God does not want
> us to be wasteful.

craft

What You Need
- duplicated page
- black construction paper
- glow-in-the-dark paint
- crayons
- blue ribbon

What to Do
1. Duplicate and cut out a light bulb, sink and song words for each child.
2. Allow the children to color the light bulbs and sinks.
3. Instruct the children to glue the bulbs, sinks and song to the construction paper sheets.
4. Assist the children in outlining the light bulbs with the glow-in-the-dark paint.
5. Show how to glue the blue ribbons to the faucets for water.
6. Sing the song to the tune of "Deep and Wide."

What To Say

It wastes electricity if you leave the light on when you aren't using it. It wastes water if you forget to turn it off after you get a drink, brush your teeth or wash your hands. We can take care of our world and be good citizens by using only as much electricity or water as we need. God wants us to be good citizens.

Good Citizen

45

A Garden Scene

bulletin board

What You Need
• duplicated pages
• poster paper
• crayons
• glue

What to Do
1. Duplicate and cut out a flower for each child.
2. Cover a wall or bulletin board with poster paper. Draw large trees on the paper.
3. Allow the children to color their flowers and stems. Show how to glue the stems to the flowers.
4. Assist in gluing the flowers to the poster paper to create a garden scene.
5. Write the memory verse along the bottom.
6. Allow the children to sit in front of the "garden" during story time.

Good Citizen

Chapter 5
God Helps Me to Be Kind

 Memory Verse

Love is kind.
1 Corinthians 13:4

Story to Share
David Is Kind to Mephibosheth

King David's best friend was Jonathan, King Saul's son. When the two were young men, they promised that they would always be friends. David also promised Jonathan that he would always take care of Jonathan's family.

Jonathan was killed in a battle with the Philistines. But King David was so busy taking care of his nation that he forgot his promise to Jonathan.

When he remembered, David instructed his men to find Jonathan's family. They found Jonathan's son, Mephibosheth, who was not able to walk because of an accident when he was a baby. Mephibosheth had grown up and married, but he lived with his family far away from other people. He didn't want people to be mean to him because of his handicap.

Mephibosheth was frightened when David invited him to the palace. He knew his grandfather, Saul, had been mean to David. Mephibosheth thought David might want to kill the other family members.

When he got to the palace, Mephibosheth bowed down before the king. He shook with fear.

"Don't be afraid," David told him. "Your father was my best friend. I won't harm you. I will give you all the land that belonged to Saul, your grandfather. I will give you everything you need."

Mephibosheth had lived away from people so long that he was shy. He felt unworthy of the honor King David was giving him. "Thank you, King David," Mephibosheth said, bowing once more. "Thank you for your kindness."

Mephibosheth lived in comfort, enjoying the land, herds and flocks King David gave to him. "King David loved my father," Mephibosheth said, "and with that love he showed kindness to me."

— Based on 2 Samuel 9

Discussion Questions

1. What promise did David make to Jonathan?
2. How can you show kindness to your friends?

game
. . . .

What You Need
• duplicated page
• crayons
• toy crown

What to Do
1. Duplicate and cut out a Mephibosheth figure for each child.
2. Allow the children to color their Mephibosheths.
3. Choose one child to wear the crown and be King David.
4. "King David" should leave the room while the rest hide their Mephibosheth figures. When King David returns, he or she should try to find all the Mephibosheths. Continue as time allows.

What to Say
Sometimes being kind isn't easy. But like King David, we should remember to find a way to be kind.

Kind

Searching for Mephibosheth

Love is kind.
1 Corinthians 13:4

48

Kool Kind Kids

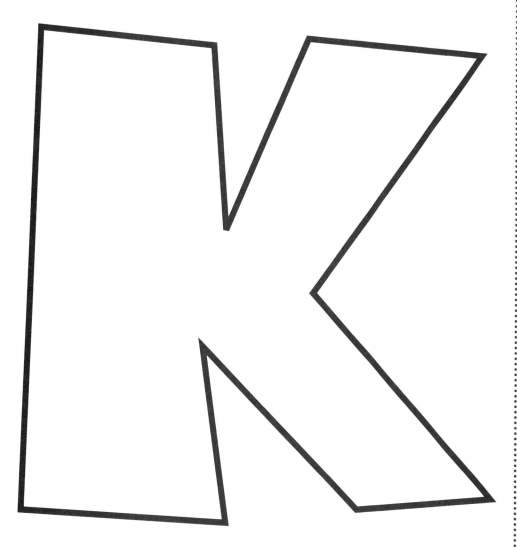

Continued on next page...

bulletin board

What You Need
- duplicated pages
- colored paper
- crayons
- picture of each child
- lettering

What to Do
1. Duplicate and cut out a picture frame for each child. Duplicate the large "Ks" on colored paper so you have enough to go around the board plus 25 extras. Cut out all the "Ks."
2. Allow the children to color their frames.
3. Attach the "Ks" around the bulletin board for a border. Using pre-made letters, attach the title "We're Kool, Kind Kids!"
4. Glue the children's pictures in their frames and attach them randomly to the board.
5. As you catch each child doing something kind, write the act and the child's name on a large "K" and attach it to the board.

Kind

Story Wheel

love is
kind

craft
. . . .
What You Need
- duplicated page
- card stock
- dessert-size paper plates
- crayons
- paper fasteners

What to Do
1. Duplicate a Story Wheel to card stock for each child.
2. Before class, cut a wedge (one-fifth of plate) from each plate.
3. Allow the children to color the Story Wheel pictures.
4. Assist the children in attaching the plates to the Story Wheels with paper fasteners.
5. Make a Story Wheel to use in telling the Bible story.
6. After the children make their own Story Wheels, allow each child to have a turn to tell the story to the others.

Kind

51

craft

What You Need
- duplicated page
- crayons
- plastic drinking straws
- tape
- bee stickers
- glue

What to Do
1. Duplicate two flowers and a leaf for each child.
2. Allow the children to color the flowers and leaves.
3. Assist each child in taping a straw to the back of one flower and gluing the back of the other flower to the taped side of the first flower.
4. Allow each child to glue the leaf around the straw.
5. Give each child a bee sticker to place on one of the flower petals.
6. Optional: Have each child make two flowers so the children can give one away and keep the other.

Kind

BEE-ing Kind Flower

Love is kind. I Cor. 13:4

What To Say

The flower shows the bee kindness by giving nectar that the bee can make into honey. We can show kindness by giving our flowers to cheer neighbors or friends.

A Song of Kindness

What You Need
- duplicated page
- wiggle eyes
- glue

What to Do
1. Duplicate and cut out a heart and smile for each child.
2. Give each child a heart and smile. Allow the children to glue the smiles and wiggle eyes to the blank sides of the hearts.
3. Write each child's name on his or her heart.
4. Sing the song to the tune of "London Bridge."
5. Instruct the children to hold their hearts and sing the song. On the second verse, each child should give his or her heart to another child. Sing the song five times and then have each child find his or her heart.

Do you know that love is kind,
love is kind, love is kind?
Do you know that love is kind?
God loves kindness.

I'll be kind and share my heart,
share my heart, share my heart.
I'll be kind and share my heart,
spreading kindness.

Showing kindness makes me smile

What To Say

Look how many were able to hold your heart!
When we show kindness to someone, it travels to another and another.
Sometimes it even comes back to us!

Kind

53

A Kingly Snack

What You Need

- duplicated page
- bright paper
- pancakes
- peanut butter
- jelly
- milk
- small foam cups
- glue
- crayons

What to Do

1. Duplicate a verse circle to bright paper for each child.
2. Before class, spread the pancakes with peanut butter and jelly. Roll each one like a jelly roll and cut into 1" pieces.
3. Allow the children to decorate their cups and glue the verse circles on the bottoms.
4. Serve the children the milk and pinwheels snack.

What to Say

When we tilt our glasses up to drink, the verse will show. Every time you see someone's verse, say, "Love is kind."

Kind

Love is kind.
1 Corinthians 13:4

Love is kind.
1 Corinthians 13:4

Love is kind.
1 Corinthians 13:4

Love is kind.
1 Corinthians 13:4

Love is kind.
1 Corinthians 13:4

Love is kind.
1 Corinthians 13:4

Color the Picture

1. red
2. blue
3. green
4. yellow
5. black
6. tan

Love is kind. 1 Corinthians 13:4

puzzle

What You Need
- duplicated page
- crayons in the colors listed on the page
- construction paper
- smiley face stickers

What to Do
1. Duplicate a picture for each child.
2. Instruct the children to color the picture using the color key. Assist as needed.
3. Allow each child to choose their construction paper color. Help each child center the picture on the construction paper and attach it with smiley stickers at all four corners.
4. If time permits, allow the children to draw pictures of themselves being kind. Attach those pictures with stickers to the backs of the sheets.

What to Say
When we are kind, it makes three people smile: you, the one to whom you showed kindness and God.

Kind

puzzle

What You Need
- duplicated page
- crayons

What to Do
1. Give each child a puzzle and a crayon.
2. Read the questions and allow the children to circle the pictures that answer the question.

What to Say
1. Who was David's best friend, Mephibosheth or Jonathan?
2. Who became king, David or Jonathan?
3. Which son of Jonathan's did David find, Michael or Mephibosheth?
4. What part of Mephibosheth's body was crippled, legs or arms?
5. What did King David give to Mephibosheth, land or a bike?

Kind

Circle the Answer

Chapter 6
God Helps Me to Be Respectful

📖 Memory Verse

Show proper respect to everyone.
1 Peter 2:17

📖 Story to Share
Come to the Party

Do you like to hear a story? Jesus knew that people like stories, so that's how He taught people. All His stories helped the people know how to live for God.

One day, Jesus told the story of a king who was preparing a big party. The party was in honor of his son's marriage. In Bible times, wedding receptions were large gatherings. If you were rich, you could invite the entire city to your party. A king's party lasted seven whole days and the king expected his guests to stay until the end. For poor people who needed to work on their land, this was a hardship. But because they respected their king, they would attend the reception if they were invited.

In Jesus' story about a king and his party, the king invited many important people.

"Tell those I have invited that everything is ready," he told the men issuing the invitation.

But when the invitations were offered to the rich people, they made excuses.

"I can't come. I need to tend to my field," said one important person.

"I can't come either," said another rich person. "I have my business to run."

"Forget the important people," the king said when he heard the excuses. "Give the invitations to the poor people. Go anywhere you can to find them. They will show respect to my son and me by coming to our reception."

The poor people did come to the party out of respect for the king. But some of them showed their disrespect by coming without wedding clothes. The king had them thrown out of the reception.

Jesus told those listening, "Just like the wedding party, there will be many who have been invited to heaven, but because they show disrespect to my heavenly Father, they will not be allowed to enter. Only those who respect God and His laws will enter heaven."

— Based on Matthew 22:1-14

❓❓ Discussion Questions

1. What excuses did the people make for not coming to the party?
2. We can show our respect for God by attending church. How else can we show our respect to God?

activity

What You Need
- duplicated page
- crayons
- magnet or hook and loop tape
- magnet or flannel board

What to Do
1. Duplicate and cut out a set of story pictures for you and for each child.
2. Allow the children to color the pictures.
3. Place magnet tape (for a magnet board) or hook and loop tape (for flannel) on the backs of the pictures.
4. Tell the story, using the pictures. Allow each child a turn at telling the story with his or her own pictures, or form teams of two and let the team members tell their stories to each other.

Respectful

Story Pictures

Party Food

What You Need
- duplicated page
- crayons
- wax paper
- angel food cake squares
- canned whipped topping
- mini M&Ms® candies

What to Do
1. Duplicate a place mat for each child.
2. Instruct children to draw their faces under the party hats. Read the top line with them, and the memory verse.
3. Allow the children to color their mats.
4. Place a sheet of wax paper on top of each mat to protect it.
5. Give each child a cake square. Allow the children to squirt topping on their cake, and sprinkle on M&Ms®.

I will be respectful.

Show proper respect to everyone.   1 Peter 2:17

What To Say

What should we say to show respect to the one who cooks our meals? (Thank you) What do we say to the One who makes it possible for us to have food to eat? (Thank you) Let's bow our heads and say "thank You" before we eat this treat.

Respectful

Give Respect

snack

What You Need
- duplicated page
- crayons

What to Do
1. Duplicate a worksheet for each child.
2. Instruct the children to draw pictures of themselves in the rectangles.
3. Discuss each authority figure and ask, "Is this someone to whom you should show respect?"
4. Instruct the children to draw lines from their pictures to the authority figures to whom they will show respect.

Respectful

pastor

father

police officer

teacher

coach

doctor

mother

fire fighter

60

Soaring Balloons

Show proper

respect to everyone.

1 Peter 2:17

A celebration!
A celebration!
Jesus invites us here
each Sunday.
We learn Good News
about God,
Sing glad praises
and applaud.
Come, join our class,
And party with us!

Continued from right...
   to repeat the threading with the "respect to everyone" balloon and the "show proper" balloon.
5. Tie a knot at the end of each child's yarn as close to the balloon as possible (if you have excess yarn, cut it off before tying the knot).
6. Show how to hold on to the straw and wave the celebration balloons.
7. Sing the Celebration Song to the tune of "Running Over." Choose a child to skip behind you (parade fashion) and wave his or her balloons. When you get to "Come, join our class," that child should choose another child to skip behind him or her. Continue until all the children are involved.

What to Say

Not all the people came to the king's great party. But that didn't stop him — he kept inviting others! Jesus wants us to invite our friends and neighbors to church, too, even if they decide not to come.

song

What You Need
- duplicated page
- plastic drinking straws
- crayons
- yarn
- chenille stems

What to Do
1. Duplicate and cut out three balloons for each child. Punch holes where indicated on the balloons. Cut yarn into 30" lengths. Tie a knot in one end of each length.
2. Allow the children to color their balloons.
3. Make a hoop at the top of a chenille stem for each child to use as a needle. Slip the yarn through the hoop and show how to slide the cleaner up through the straw.
4. Instruct each child to remove the chenille stem and thread the yarn through the bottom hole of the verse reference balloon to the back and out the top hole. Allow them

Continued at left...

Respectful

Party Invitation

craft

What You Need
- duplicated page
- crayons
- heart stickers

What to Do
1. Fill in the blanks with appropriate information, then duplicate a party invitation for each child.
2. Let each child color an invitation.
3. Show how to attach the heart stickers to the tops of the pictured strings for balloons.
4. If possible, take the children on a walk to hand out the invitations around the neighborhood or at a park.

Respectful

It's Party Time!

Come Celebrate with us

and learn about Jesus!

when _____

where _____

Show proper respect to everyone. 1 Peter 2:17

Perfect Attendance

bulletin board

What You Need
- duplicated page
- crayons
- yarn
- construction paper

What to Do
1. Duplicate a church and child marker for each child.
2. Allow the children to color their churches and markers.
3. Allow each child to glue the church to construction paper.
4. Go around and cut 1½" slits in each stone of the walkways.
5. Demonstrate how the child markers can be inserted in the slits.

This child wants to attend church every Sunday. Let's put him in the first stone. When you come to church, move him to the next space. Can you get the boy to the church? You can if you come every Sunday!

In the story, the king invited many people to his party, but they were disrespectful and didn't go. God invites us to gather to learn about Him. Let's be respectful and go to church each week.

Continued on next page...

Respectful

63

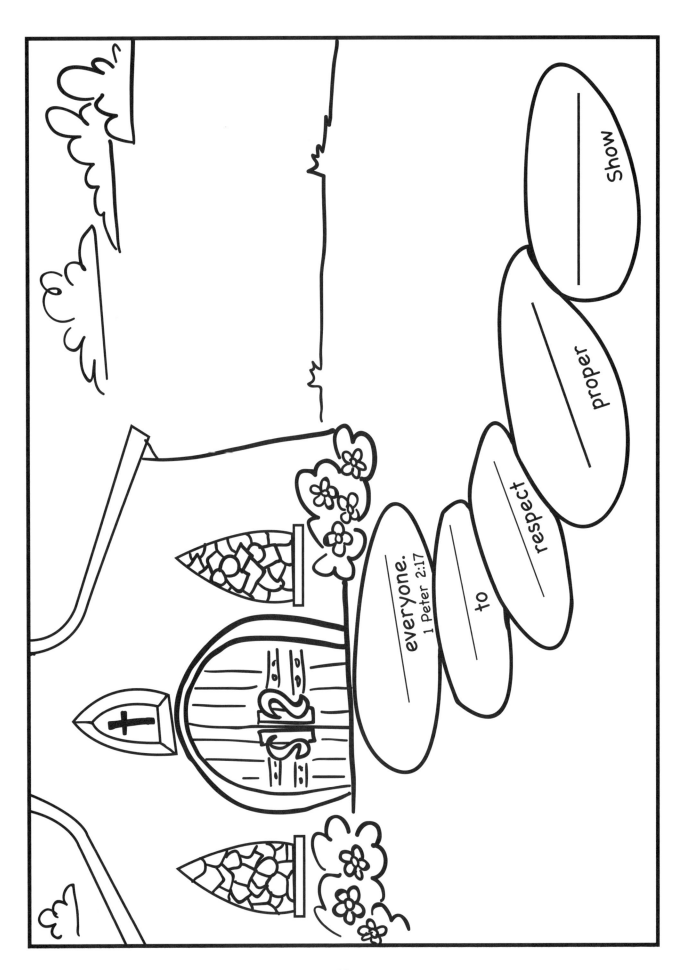

Show

proper

respect

to

everyone.
1 Peter 2:17

What's the Gift?

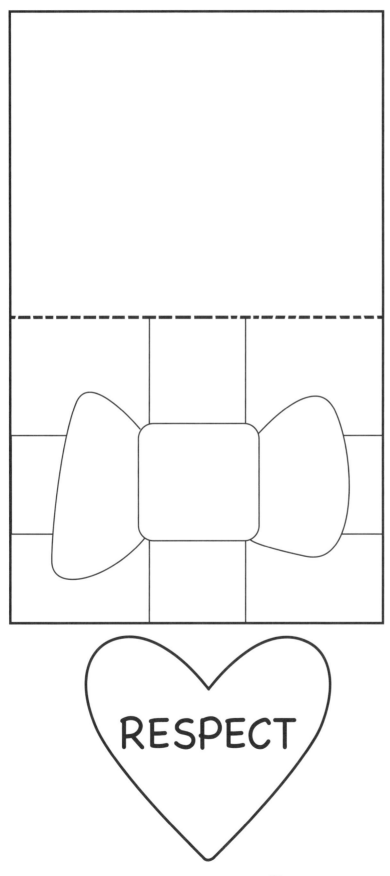

RESPECT

What You Need
• duplicated page
• crayons
• glue
• gift bows

What to Do
1. Duplicate a gift and heart for each child.
2. Allow the children to color their gifts and hearts.
3. Instruct the children to fold the gifts on the dashed lines.
4. Show where to glue the heart inside the gift.
5. Give each child a bow to put on his or her gift.
6. Demonstrate how to lift the "lid" to see the gift we can give others.

Respectful

Party Hat

craft

What You Need
- duplicated page
- construction paper
- decorative-edge scissors
- glue
- smile stickers
- crayons
- clear tape
- stapler

What to Do
1. Trace the triangle on construction paper and cut one for each child. Also cut an 11" x 2" strip for each one.
2. Duplicate the heart patterns on colored paper and cut them out with decorative-edge scissors.
3. Tell the children to glue the hearts to the triangles.
4. Allow the children to decorate their hats using crayons and smile stickers.
5. Staple one end of a strip to a triangle. Measure the strip to the child's head and staple the other end of the strip to the triangle. Cut off excess, then cover the staples with tape.

Respectful

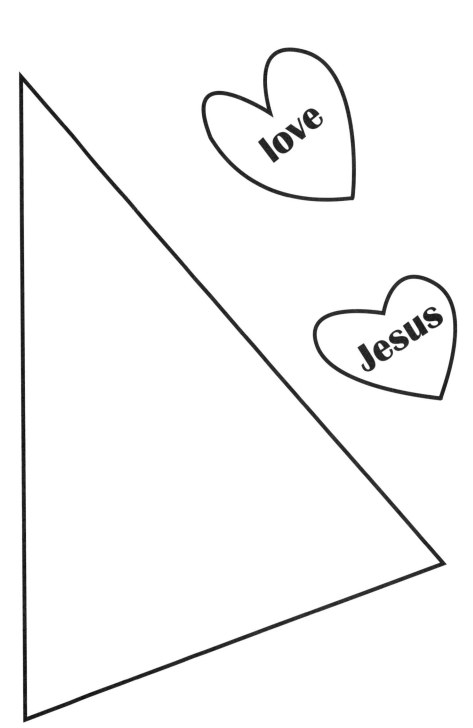

Chapter 7
God Helps Me to Be Responsible

📖 Memory Verse

Guard what has been entrusted to your care.
1 Timothy 6:20

📖 Story to Share
A Responsible Prisoner

Joseph's father, Jacob, gave him a wonderful coat. The coat was colorful – like a rainbow! The coat made Joseph feel special. But the coat made Joseph's brothers jealous. They all wanted a coat just like Joseph's.

So the brothers did something wicked to Joseph. They took his coat and sold Joseph to traders who were traveling to faraway lands. The traders took Joseph to Egypt, where he became a slave.

One day, the slave master's wife told a terrible lie about Joseph. The master believed his wife, and Joseph was put in prison. Even though Joseph did not like being in prison, he asked God to help him be cheerful. Knowing God was with him – even in prison – made Joseph's heart happy.

It didn't take the jailer long to notice how happy Joseph was. He saw how Joseph sang to calm a tired prisoner. He also saw how Joseph gave some of his food to another prisoner who was hungry. The jailer knew Joseph could be trusted.

"Joseph," the jailer said, "I am going to make you head of the prison."

Joseph was happy for the job the jailer gave him. He was responsible and worked hard to take care of the prisoners. Each morning, he took water and cloths to the prisoners so they could wash.

When the prisoners asked how he could be so happy, Joseph told them, "My God is with me."

Joseph was faithful to God and responsible to his job. So God worked through Joseph to explain people's dreams to them.

When the king of Egypt had a dream he couldn't figure out, he called Joseph. Joseph explained Pharaoh's dream. The Pharaoh was so thankful to Joseph that he made him a great leader in Egypt.

God was happy with Joseph because he was responsible and did his work well. God wants us to be responsible and do our jobs well, too.

— Based on Genesis 37-41

❓❓ Discussion Questions

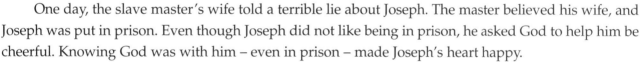

1. How was Joseph able to be happy even though he had to work hard?
2. What kinds of responsibilities do you have? (pick up toys, feed pets, set the table, etc.) What kind of attitude does God want you to have when you do them?

"Just Like Joseph" Mirror

song

What You Need
- duplicated page
- card stock
- aluminum foil
- crayons
- glue

What to Do
1. Duplicate a mirror on card stock and cut out one for each child.
2. Duplicate and cut out a Joseph for each child.
3. Trace around the center of the mirror for a pattern. Use the pattern to cut a foil mirror for each child.
4. Allow the children to color their Josephs.
5. Assist the children in gluing the foil to the card stock mirrors and the Josephs to the mirrors.
6. Sing the song to the tune of "Three Blind Mice." Tell the children to look in the mirror when the song says, "Just like Joseph."

Responsible

Just like Joseph,
Just like Joseph,
I want to be,
I want to be.
Like Joseph I'll be responsible,
Doing my chores is my number one rule.
Just like Joseph, I want to be,
Just like Joseph,
Just like Joseph.

68

Stained Glass Coat

craft

What You Need
- duplicated page
- card stock
- washable markers
- empty spray bottle
- water
- coffee filters
- clear, self-stick plastic
- raffia, ribbon or yarn

What to Do
1. Make several copies of the pattern on card stock. Cut out the centers (coats) to make stencils.
2. Allow each child to color a coffee filter with the markers.
3. Help the children spray the filters with the water. Let the filters dry.
4. Instruct the children to trace around the coat stencils on the filters.
5. Help the children cover the coats with clear plastic.
6. Punch a hole at the top of each coat and thread with raffia. Tie in a bow for hanging.

What To Say

Even though Joseph lost his beautiful coat, he was determined to be responsible. When he was in prison, he was the best prisoner he could be. When he became a leader in Egypt, he was the best leader he could be. Joseph was responsible because he wanted to make God happy.

Responsible

69

Joseph's Wardrobe

craft

What You Need
- duplicated page
- crayons
- gold glitter glue

What to Do
1. Before class, make a set of pictures to use in telling the story.
2. Duplicate and cut out a Joseph and a set of clothes for each child.
3. Allow the children to color Joseph and his clothes.
4. Assist the children in adding glue glitter to Joseph's Egyptian robe.
5. Allow the students to take turns retelling the Bible story.

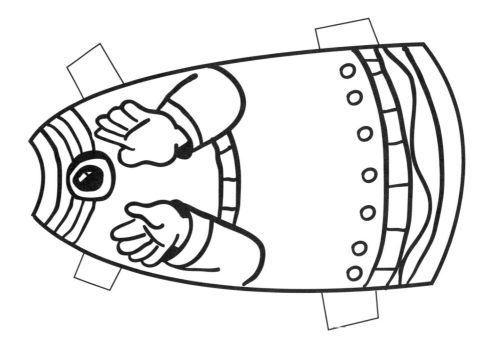

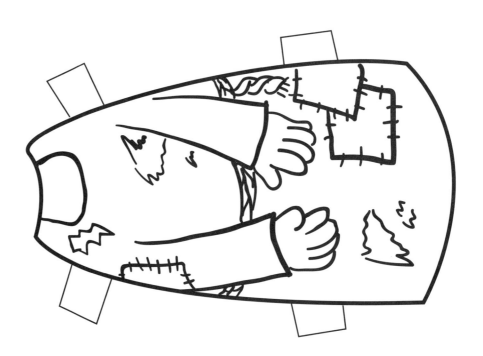

Responsible

Guard Puppet

What You Need
- duplicated page
- crayons
- paper lunch sacks
- glue
- gray construction paper

What to Do

1. Duplicate and cut out a set of guard puppet pieces for each child.
2. Cut gray construction paper into ½" x 3" strips.
3. Allow the children to color the puppet pieces.
4. Assist each child in gluing the puppet pieces to paper sacks.
5. Demonstrate how to make a chain with six paper strips.
6. Assist the children in gluing the chains' ends in place on the puppets' hands.
7. Allow the children to practice the verse using their puppets.

Responsible

What To Say

Just like a guard watches his prisoners, we should be responsible for what God gives us. If your responsibility is to make your bed each morning, don't miss a day of making your bed. If your responsibility is to take out the trash, watch the trash can so you'll know when the bag is full and ready to go. Guard your responsibilities!

Chore Chart

_____'s Chore Chart

Guard what has been entrusted to your care. 1 Timothy 6:20

Sunday	Monday	Tuesday	Wednesday	Thursday	Friday	Saturday

craft

What You Need
- duplicated page
- crayons
- white vinegar
- non-toxic white glue
- snack-size plastic bags
- cotton swabs

What to Do
1. Duplicate and cut out a chore chart and seven dustpans for each child.
2. Pre-mix 1 part vinegar and 2 parts glue.
3. Let children color the chore charts and dustpans.
4. Instruct the children to spread the glue mixture on the backs of the dustpans using cotton swabs. Let dry.
5. Show how to put the dustpans in plastic bags to take home.

What to Say
Use your chart to remember to be responsible. After doing your chores each day, moisten the back of a dustpan and stick it to the chart.

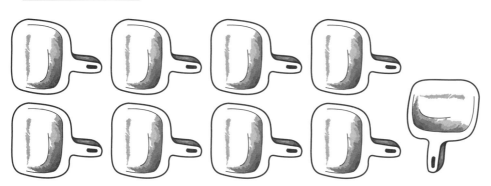

Responsible

Pet Care Puzzle

puzzle
· · · · · · · · · · ·

What You Need
• duplicated page
• crayons

What to Do
1. Duplicate a worksheet for each child.
2. Instruct the children to draw a line from each animal to the picture which shows proper care of that animal.
3. Allow the children to color the pictures.

What to Say
Having a pet is a big responsibility. What are some of the chores you might have with a pet? (feeding, watering, keeping it clean, making sure it has the shots it needs)

Responsible

Chewing Gum Responsibility

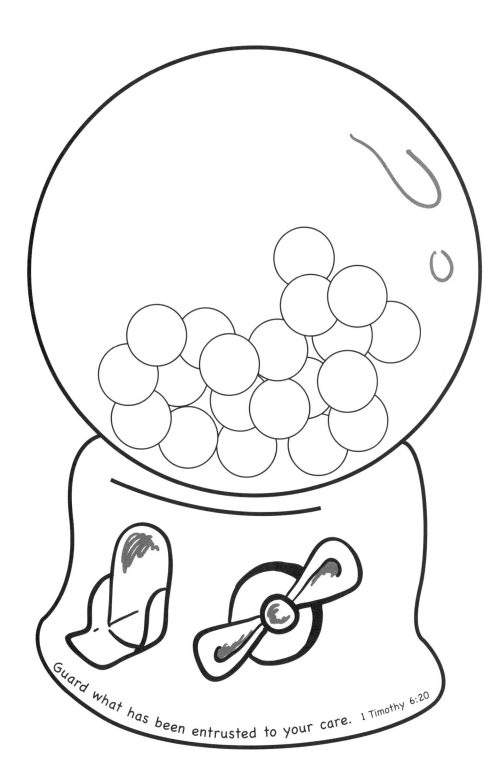

Guard what has been entrusted to your care. 1 Timothy 6:20

craft

What You Need
- duplicated page
- crayons
- round colored stickers

What to Do
1. Duplicate a gum machine picture for each child.
2. Allow the children to color their gum machines.
3. Instruct the children to place a round sticker on every gumball.

What to Say
When we chew gum, we are responsible for placing our chewed gum in the trash. You can wrap it in a piece of paper or tissue so it won't stick to the side of the can. God wants you to be responsible. When you act in a responsible way, you make God happy!

Responsible

Rainbow Buttons

snack

What You Need
- duplicated page
- crayons
- clear, self-stick plastic
- cream cheese
- food coloring
- round crackers
- plastic knives

What to Do
1. Duplicate a coat for each child.
2. Pre-mix food coloring into five cups of cream cheese.
3. Allow the children to color their coats with crayons.
4. Go around and cover the coats with clear plastic.
5. Allow the children to spread the cream cheese on the crackers to make rainbow buttons for their coats.

Responsible

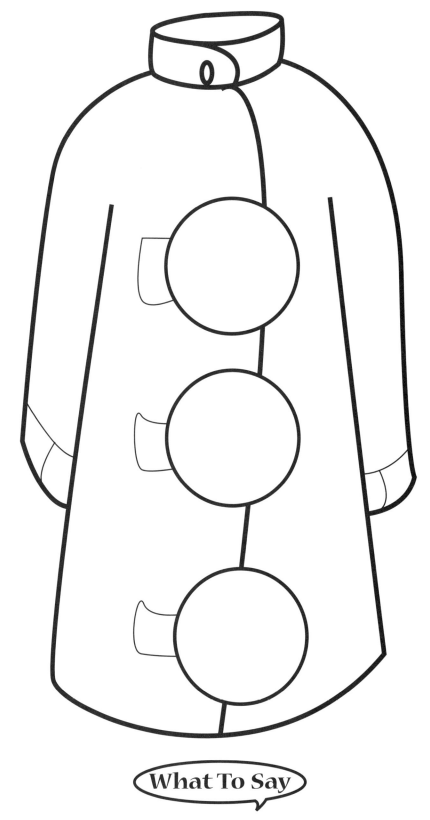

What To Say

Joseph's coat was given to him by his father. When your mommy or daddy provides clothing for you, remember to take care of it by folding it in your drawer or handing it in the closet.

76

Chapter 8
God Helps Me to Be Trustworthy

Memory Verse

These men were considered trustworthy.
Nehemiah 13:13

Story to Share
Trustworthy Philemon

In Bible times, many people owned slaves. The slaves had to work in their masters' fields and homes. Some slaves were used to run errands and even were trusted to handle money for their masters.

If a slave ran away from his owner, he received severe punishment. If someone found a runaway slave, he was required to send the slave back to his master.

When Paul was in prison, he met a slave named Onesimus. The name Onesimus means "useful". Onesimus was the slave of one of Paul's friends, Philemon. Onesimus had run away. Paul knew he had to send him back, but Onesimus had been so kind to Paul that it made Paul sad to think Onesimus would be punished for running away.

Many people believed slaves were lazy and undisciplined. Paul wanted Philemon to know that Onesimus had been very useful, just as his name says. Paul had helped Onesimus to become a Christian. Paul wanted Philemon to know that he now could trust Onesimus because Onesimus had changed his ways. So Paul got out his writing paper and pen, and wrote a letter to Philemon.

"Philemon, my dear friend," he wrote, "I am writing to you about your slave Onesimus. He has been useful to me and I would like to keep him here, but I am sending him back to you as the law requires.

"Onesimus is now a Christian brother, and I hope you accept him as one. You are trustworthy. I know you will do even more than what I ask."

Philemon was happy to welcome back Onesimus, not with punishment but with love. Paul knew Philemon could be trusted to do the right thing, and he was right. Philemon was trustworthy.

— Based on Philemon

Discussion Questions

1. Paul knew Philemon could be trusted to do the right thing. Can you be trusted to do right?
2. Who changed Onesimus' heart to make him free from sin?

Banana Coin

snack
· · · · · · · · · · ·

What You Need
• duplicated page
• crayons
• non-toxic white glue
• napkins
• bananas
• cream cheese
• peanut butter
• wax paper

What to Do
1. Duplicate and cut out a place mat and Onesimus figure for each child.
2. Allow the children to color the place mats.
3. Assist in spreading a thin layer of glue on the place mats' dashed lines. Instruct the children to press the Onesimus figures into the glue. Allow to dry.
4. Cover each mat with wax paper.
5. Give each child a napkin, six banana "coins" (sliced bananas) to lay on their mat, and a small container of peanut butter or cream cheese for dipping.

Trustworthy

What To Say

Paul knew Onesimus was trustworthy. He offered to pay Onesimus's debt to Philemon. When you eat the coins, remember it was Jesus who changed Onesimus' heart and made him trustworthy.

I am trustworthy

These men were considered trustworthy. nehemiah 13:13

craft

What You Need
- duplicated page
- pencils
- crayons

What to Do
1. Duplicate and cut out a storybook for each child. Fold the book on the dashed lines.
2. Read the title and book to the children.
3. Allow the children to color the pictures.
4. If time permits, allow the children to pair up with friends and tell the story to each other.

Trustworthy

Ethan and Emily's Mini Book

Being trustworthy makes us happy!

We like to play but we'll do what we said.

Ethan and Emily are trustworthy.

These men were considered trustworthy. nehemiah 13:13

We will pick up our toys, Mommy.

Bible Story Bookmark

craft

What You Need
- duplicated page
- crayons
- glue
- yarn
- hole punch

What to Do
1. Duplicate and cut out a bookmark and pictures for each child.
2. Allow the children to color the pictures.
3. Instruct the children to glue the pictures in the following order on their bookmarks: Onesimus runs, Paul writes, and Philemon welcomes back Onesimus.
4. Assist in punching holes where indicated.
5. Cut yarn in 8" lengths. Tie each piece of yarn through a bookmark hole for a tassel.
6. Retell the Bible story, allowing the children to point to the correct pictures on their bookmarks.

Trustworthy

Clock Verse Review

game

• • • • • • • • • • • • •

What You Need
• duplicated page
• paper fasteners
• crayons

What to Do
1. Duplicate and cut out a clock and hands for each child.
2. Allow the children to color their clocks.
3. Assist in attaching the hands to the clocks with paper fasteners.
4. Use the hands on the clock to review the verse. Even though most of the children will not be able to read the words, they can move the hands to each word and "read" the verse with you.

What to Say
Being on time is a way to show you are trustworthy.

Trustworthy

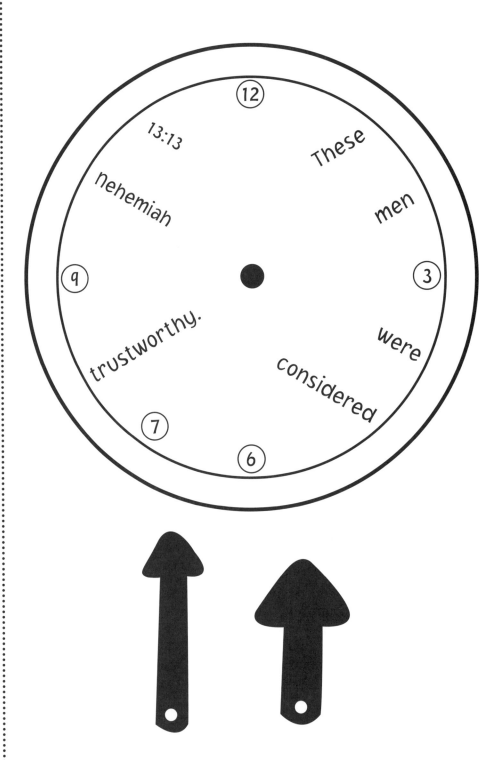

Trustworthy Brushing

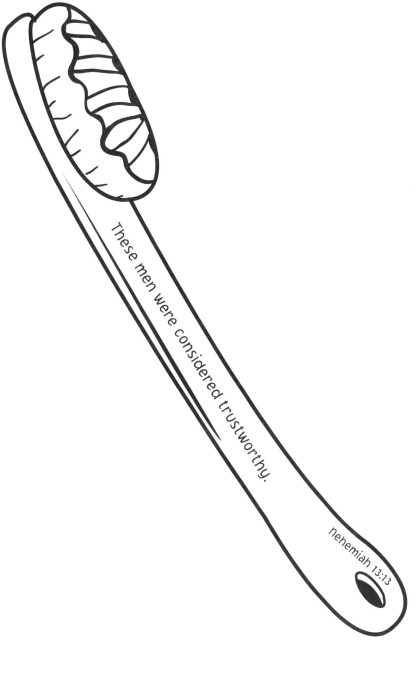

These men were considered trustworthy.

Nehemiah 13:13

craft

What You Need
- duplicated page
- card stock
- hole punch
- white felt
- glue
- small smile stickers

What to Do
1. Duplicate a toothbrush to cardstock for each child.
2. Cut out a piece of white felt to go over each set of bristles.
3. Punch a hole at the end of each handle where indicated.
4. Allow the children to color their toothbrushes.
5. Instruct the children to glue the felt bristles onto their brushes.
6. Give each child five stickers to take home.

What To Say

The dentist says we should brush our teeth every day. We show we are trustworthy when we do what the dentist asks, even though the dentist can't see if we obey. Each day you brush your teeth this week, put a sticker on the handle of this toothbrush.

Trustworthy

puzzle

What You Need
- duplicated page
- pencils

What to Do

1. Duplicate a worksheet for each child.
2. Read the description of the first situation that is pictured, then read the two solutions. Discuss which is the trustworthy thing to do. Instruct the children to circle the correct picture.
3. Continue with the other two situations.

Amanda promises to sweep the porch.
a) Amanda watches video.
b) Amanda sweeps the porch.

Ryan finds a dollar.
a) Ryan puts the dollar in the offering.
b) Ryan puts the dolllar in his piggy bank.

Kyle breaks Amanda's teapot.
a) Kyle tells Amanda he's sorry.
b) Kyle hides the pieces under his bed.

Trustworthy

Find the Paths

puzzle

What You Need
- duplicated page
- crayons

What to Do
1. Duplicate a puzzle for each child.
2. Instruct the children to use red crayons and find the path to Paul, starting at Onesimus.
3. Then the children should use green crayons to help Onesimus find the path from Paul back to his owner, Philemon.

Answer key is on page 87

Onesimus

Paul

Philemon

song

What You Need
- duplicated page
- large craft sticks
- crayons
- glue

What to Do
1. Duplicate a song sign for each child.
2. Allow the children to color the signs.
3. Assist each child in gluing a craft stick to the back of his or her sign.
4. Sing the song to the tune of "Stop and Let Me Tell You." Each time you say, "Stand," stomp your left foot, and each time you say, "Firm," stomp your right foot.

Trustworthy

"Trustworthy" Song

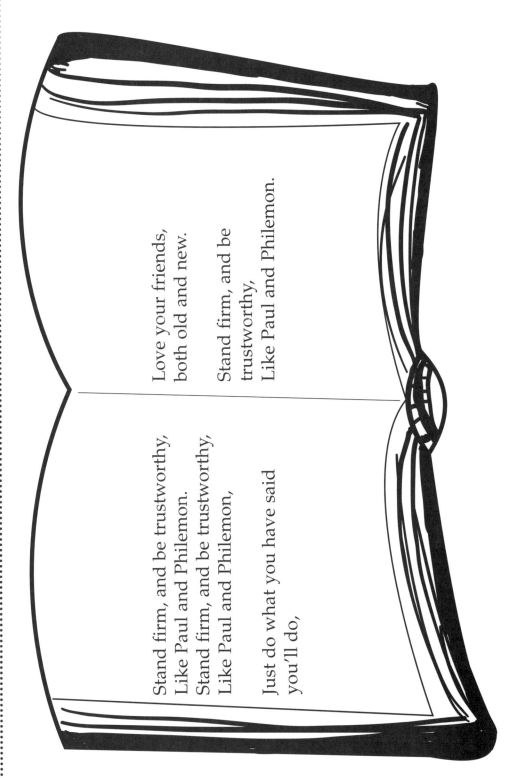

Love your friends,
both old and new.

Stand firm, and be
trustworthy,
Like Paul and Philemon.

Stand firm, and be trustworthy,
Like Paul and Philemon.
Stand firm, and be trustworthy,
Like Paul and Philemon,

Just do what you have said
you'll do,

Onesimus

Paul

Philemon

*Answer key for the
Find the Paths puzzle
on page 84*

Parent Letter

teacher help

What You Need
- duplicated page

What to Do
1. Duplicate a supply letter for each family in your church. (Even families who do not have children might be happy to help with class materials.)
2. Fold each letter in thirds and seal with a sticker.

From the Room Border *on next page...*

Miscellaneous

Dear Parents and Friends of our Preschool Class,

We are making Bible crafts in our preschool class. If you have or can purchase any of the items below, they would be appreciated. We'll put your donations toward making masterpieces!

- buttons
- chenille stems
- clear, self-stick plastic
- construction paper
- crepe paper
- gift bows
- glow-in-the-dark glue
- glue
- gold glitter glue
- hook and loop tape
- magnet tape
- paper lunch sacks
- plastic drinking straws
- spring-type clothespins
- stickers: smiley faces, hearts and miscellaneous
- yarn, trim and fabric scraps

Thank you,

_____

Preschool Teacher

trustworthy

Room Border

God
helps
me
to be...

compassionate

fair

forgiving

bulletin board
. . . .

What You Need
- duplicated pages
- fluorescent paper
- crayons

What to Do
1. Duplicate the "God Helps Me to Be…" rectangles to white paper and the character traits to fluorescent paper.
2. Allow the children to color the "God Helps Me to Be…" rectangles.
3. Attach the border to the walls around your classroom, alternating the "God Helps Me to Be…" with the character traits.

Continued on previous page and next page...

Miscellaneous

a good citizen

kind

respectful

responsible

Wiggle Buster

activity

What You Need
• duplicated page

What to Say

Look at my hands
(wiggle hands)
Look at my nose
(wrinkle nose)
Look at my mouth
(open mouth
wide)
Look at my toes.
(hold up leg and
wiggle toes)

God made them all
(point to God)
Now I can be
(arms wide then
point to self)
A great kid for Him
(jump)
Because God Helps
Me!
(arms and legs
wide spread)

Miscellaneous

craft

What You Need
- duplicated page
- card stock
- crayons
- wiggle eyes
- ribbons
- glue

What to Do
1. Duplicate a child's face and verse strip to card stock for each child. Cut off the ponytails for the boys.
2. Allow the children to color the faces to look like themselves.
3. Give each child two wiggle eyes to glue on.
4. Assist the girls in tying ribbons and gluing them on the ponytails.
5. Assist each child in cutting out the mouth, to leave a hole in its place.
6. Cut two 1" x 3" strips from card stock for each child. Assist each child in gluing two strips across the mouth on the the back of the

Continued at right...

Continued at right...

Miscellaneous

Verse Review

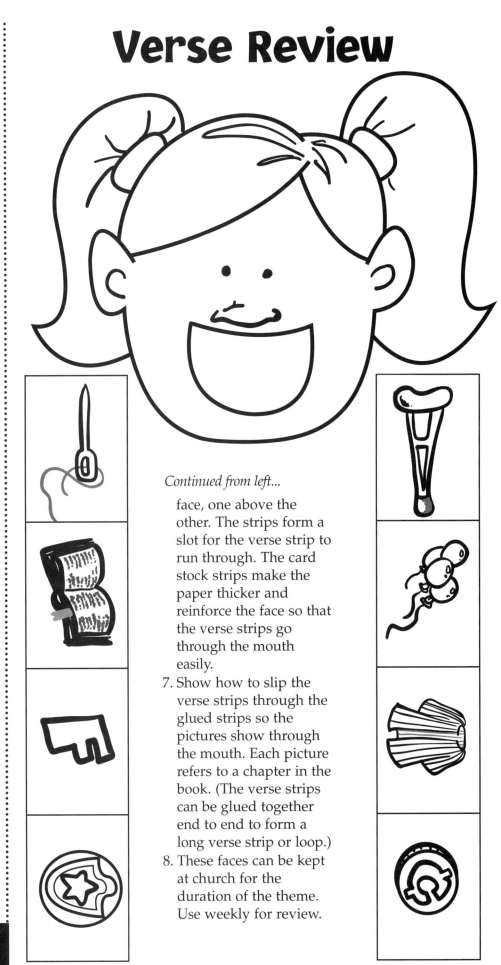

Continued from left...

Continued from left...

face, one above the other. The strips form a slot for the verse strip to run through. The card stock strips make the paper thicker and reinforce the face so that the verse strips go through the mouth easily.

7. Show how to slip the verse strips through the glued strips so the pictures show through the mouth. Each picture refers to a chapter in the book. (The verse strips can be glued together end to end to form a long verse strip or loop.)
8. These faces can be kept at church for the duration of the theme. Use weekly for review.

Post-a-Note

What You Need
- duplicated page
- heavy paper
- crayons

What to Do
1. Duplicate the post-a-note to heavy paper.
2. Lay out the notes and crayons for early arrivals to color.
3. On the back middle section of each note, print an absentee child's name and address.
4. Write a short personal note on the inside and allow the children to sign their names.
5. Place a stamp on the outside and close the note with a sticker.

Miscellaneous

Take-home Certificate

teacher help

What You Need
- duplicated page
- crayons
- glue
- perfect attendance stickers

What to Do
1. Duplicate and cut out a certificate and a boy or girl for each child. (Cut off the ponytails for the boys.)
2. Before class, fill in the blank lines on the certificates.
3. Allow each child to color a boy or girl.
4. Instruct the children to glue their boys or girls to the space indicated on the certificates.
5. If a child has perfect attendance, give him or her a sticker to attach to the bottom left of the certificate.

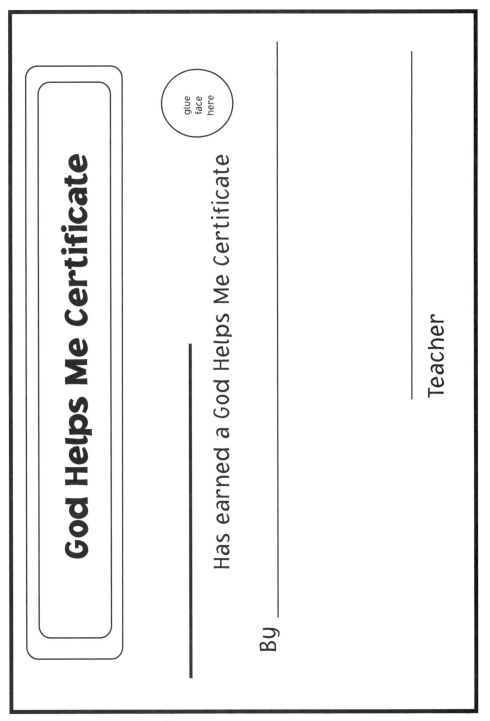

God Helps Me Certificate

glue face here

Has earned a God Helps Me Certificate

Teacher

By

Attendance Chain

compassionate,
fair, forgiving,
a good citizen,
kind, respectful,
responsible, and
trustworthy

teacher help

. . . .

What You Need
- duplicated page
- decorative-edged scissors
- yarn
- hole punch
- crayons

What to Do
1. Duplicate a set of hearts for each child.
2. Punch a hole at the top of one heart per set. Thread a length of yarn through the hole and tie the ends together. Write the character trait names on each heart in the set.
3. As the children arrive, give each child his or her first heart.
4. Allow the children to decorate their hearts with crayons.
5. Make hanging chains of hearts by adding new hearts, with the new week's trait, each week the children attend. To form a chain, slide the inside heart flap through the back of the one before it.

Miscellaneous

teacher help

What You Need
- duplicated page
- craft pins with safety backs
- bold marker

What to Do
1. Before beginning the series, duplicate and cut out one tag for each student.
2. Throughout the series, watch for children in class who are fair, kind, responsible, etc.
3. On a tag, write the character trait you caught the student emulating.
4. Glue a craft pin to the tag and attach to the student's shirt.

What to Say
I saw (Grace) picking up her trash and putting it in the trash can. Wasn't that responsible of her? I saw (Jose) waiting until I was finished talking to ask his question. Wasn't that respectful of him?

Catch Them Being Good!